GREAT
FOR YOUR
BOAT

CHRIS SOUTHWOOD

Copyright © Chris Southwood
210220 12854

All rights reserved. No part of this book may be reproduced in any form or means other than for fair comment or review without permission in writing from the author.
mail@ChrisSouthwood.com

About me: I live mostly on my yacht, DriKé, in Andalusia, southern Spain. She is a 53 ft steel ketch built in Kent, England, in 1984.
During my time on board I have added loads of ideas and innovations - I share these with you in this book. I hope you enjoy.

Visit my website https://www.chrissouthwood.com/steel-ketch-drike/

Justification

Now for the usual disclaimer.

All the ideas in this book I have used on my own yacht.

With good interpretation, adaption to your boat and common sense, they will work well for you.

Check with your own professional marine engineer if you have any doubts as to the feasibility of installing these ideas.

Safe and happy sailing.

Chris Southwood

Contents

A SUPER RADIO CONTROLLED ELECTRIC PASSERELLE

One of the greatest security weakness on a boat when moored stern or bows to, Mediterranean style, is the passerelle or boarding ladder. Often this is held up from the quayside with just a few turns of the halyard around a cleat.

To any opportunist thief this sends out a clear message:
"Hey, I am not on-board, that is obvious because the passerelle has been secured from the quayside - this is so simple to untie and lower, so be my guest, undo it and come and take look around".

What spurred me to devise a solution was when a fellow sailor was trying to return some borrowed items and found I was not on board. It took him only a few seconds to work out how to lower the passerelle. He then walked around and poked the items through a partially opened hatch.
All this was in broad daylight: his access was unfettered and unchallenged.
Okay, I knew this person, but it was still an unnerving experience when I returned to find someone had been on my boat without my permission and with such ease.

So, I set about thinking how to make my boat, my home, more secure.

Heavy Shopping, heavy Passerelle. All easy by Push Button

A passerelle that was lifted via a radio control would be perfect. However, a commercially available radio controlled, motorised lifting passerelles are very expensive.

I applied some research and thought and I came up with a solution that cost me about €150 - as against thousands. It took me a couple of days to install. Ten years on, it still works well and is, for me and my crew, indispensable.

I have since installed several of these for fellow yachtsman around the marina.

Basically, there are two sets of components to buy mostly from my favourite toy-shop - eBay:

An electrical box
and four 2-way, 5-pin, relays with mounting sockets. Plus a few switches, fuses and cable.

A motor: 12 or 24 volts.

The ideal unit is a wheelchair motor or, in fact, any motor or system that is used in hospitals for lifting patients will work as they are powerful and quiet. These are normally 24 volts. Not a problem if you only have 12 volts as I have installed several into a 12-volt system. It just means they turn more slowly - they are after all used to working with variable voltage when in use in a wheelchair which may be of benefit when you arrange the lifting geometry and pulley size. Any sort of motor that is designed to lift loads will work.

If you can find one an 'Ottobok' 24-volt wheelchair motor running on 12 or 24 volts and are almost perfect for silence and power.

Electromagnet Brake

They, like most other wheelchair motors, have a built-in electromagnetic brake. The purpose is to lock the motor when not running thus applying a brake to the wheelchair.

When energy is applied to the motor, the electromagnet is simultaneously energised and de-activates the brake so the motor is free to turn.

On a wheelchair, that means when power is stopped, or there is a fault in the power supply, the wheelchair does not roll down a slope. This is obviously useful in our setup in that, when the passerelle is raised, it does not lower under gravity when the motor is no longer running.

These brakes are nearly always 12 volts. This is simple - you wire the brake in parallel with the motor when on a 12-volt system. On a 24-volt system, you will need a separate supply to the brake - best operated via a 24-volt relay in parallel with the motor if you have a 12-volt supply or, more simply, a 24-12-volt reducer. Look at the end of this book for details of these very useful units.

If the brake voltage is not marked, then try it out on the bench with 12 volts. If it does not engage with a positive click, then try with 24 volts— then you have your answer.

For the pulley drum, I used with the Ottobok a section of 25mm stainless steel tube with an 'interference fit' on the existing shaft and keyway - sounds posh but basically, I hammered it on over the keyway with some hefty whacks. I then fabricated two pulley cheeks from some scrap fibre-glass.

On one prototype, I used a 12-volt winch motor - the type you see on Landrovers and other 4x4's. You can get these on eBay, brand new, for about €50. But they are noisy! If that's not a problem then they are ideal - they are powerful, with a small footprint and they are cheap.

However, I still recommend you persevere and search eBay and other second-hand markets and try to get a good second-hand wheelchair motor - your neighbours will appreciate it.

Remember, these motors are now almost retired compared to life in a wheelchair so they are taking it easy. They only have to work for a few minutes a day and will never even get warm. So long as they are kept dry, they will last a long time.

(3) Finally, a radio control unit.

Search for this on eBay. (It will probably come from China - it will almost certainly be made there, so allow a few weeks to arrive).

Choose a unit that has a 'learning button'. This means you can add more remotes as you need them as, unfortunately, in a seawater environment, you may need to replace them occasionally. Plus, at the outset, you will need one for each member of the crew.
You can buy 'cloning fobs' but they can be a total hassle to clone - so a unit with a memory button is best.

You will also note these come in two frequencies - 433 MHz and 315 MHz. They are not interchangeable.

Technically 315Mhz is not allowed in Europe, while both 315Mhz and 433Mhz are allowed in the USA, so 433Mhz would be a better choice in a correct world as, put politically, they are a worldwide frequency that can be used everywhere.

That said, I have never seen frequency police here in Spain so I am not that worried - choice, therefore, depends on what is available.

Typical Radio control fob

However, 433 MHz is supposed to have a longer range than 315 MHz although I have not noticed this in practice - I think it depends more on the quality of the unit and the installation.

You also need to make sure the model you buy is of the correct type - you will need the one that has 'momentary contact' not 'latching'. Some on the market have the ability to change this arrangement with 'jumpers' (small tabs to connect or disconnect parts of the circuit.)

If you are worried about buying the correct bits visit my website www.ChrisSouthwood.com

I plan to add some items later in the year that I will supply direct via drop-shipping.

Scroll to boats and look at the submenu for 'Electric Passerelle Bits'.

Sure, you could buy cheaper direct but I will get you the correct parts for you.

To follow is the wiring diagram for the relays and radio control.

Passerelle Wiring Diagram Using 4 SPDT relays
See text for specifications

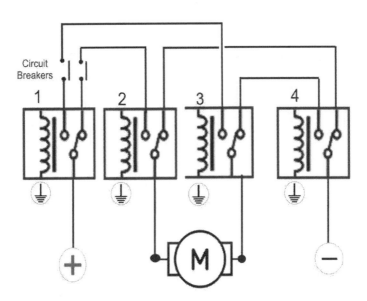

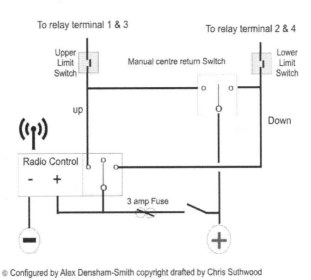

© Configured by Alex Densham-Smith copyright drafted by Chris Suthwood

The preceding is a rugged circuit using four SPDT (Single pole, double throw) relays. I suggest around 30-40-amp load capacity.

You can buy these relays with a built in LED. The lights can be helpful when setting up and if any remain on when the motor is not running, will indicate a potential fault somewhere in your system requiring investigation.

With this circuit, there is a built-in safety factor should a relay fail and fuse the contact points – as can happen with heavy inductive loads like a motor. As each motion – up or down – is controlled via two relays in series, the chance of simultaneous failure is minimal. Also, there are separate circuit breakers to each up/down circuit.

If the 'up' circuit, for example, developed a fault and tripped out a breaker, then one can still lower the passerelle as it is independently fused and wired.

The amperage of the circuit breakers is important. Too low and they will trip too soon. Too high and there could be some damage if there is a fault in a pair of relays (unlikely) – around 5-10 amps would be about right. However, this will depend on the wattage of the motor, the load (depending on the gearing and geometry) and the voltage.

If you are unsure, instead of initially fitting circuit breakers, install simple replaceable fuses' and experiment to see at what point they blow and move up one size – when satisfied change back to circuit breakers of similar amperage.

Locate the receiver somewhere dry and away from the motor itself. I'll explain why later *

The final consideration is the lifting mechanism. As your passerelle was almost certainly originally lifted by a halyard, then we need to find a place to mount the motor, with a drum, to wind the said passerelle up into the yonder.

On a couple of yachts I have worked on, including mine, there was room in a small cupboard located in the cabin under the mizzenmast. If not, then a teak, plastic or fibreglass box could be constructed and mounted on the deck at the foot the mast - or even on the mast itself.

Mount a good-sized electrical box that will house the relay and a few junction blocks and switches. You could put in a few LEDs - power on, radio on - that sort of stuff - so it looks cool and techie, but not essential. The relays and radio control should be separately fused at around 3 amps

If you are installing on a yacht with only 24 volts available, then you will need a 'step-down' inverter to convert 24 volts to 12 volts for the relays and radio control. These are cheap. A few euros on eBay or via me. At the end of the book, I have added more details and specs about these units.

Work out the location of the motor. You will need to experiment with the pulley system, or make up something if the motors do not have one. It need not be elaborate. I have made one from plywood with four bolts to act as the drum. Simple and effective.

There are three variables for the lifting speed when setting this up.

(1) The speed of the motor after gearing.
Around 50-120 rpm after gearing and under load is about right.

(2) The diameter of the drum
Obviously the bigger the drum, the faster it will lift the passerelle. Allow for the fact that, as the halyard is wound, the working diameter of the drum increases. The drum should accommodate around two metres of the halyard.

(3) The halyard attachment points on the passerelle
Obviously the further to the ends of the passerelle, the slower it will lift and vice-versa.

Aim to juggle all those parameters to give a lift of about 1 metre of halyard in around 5 seconds when under load.

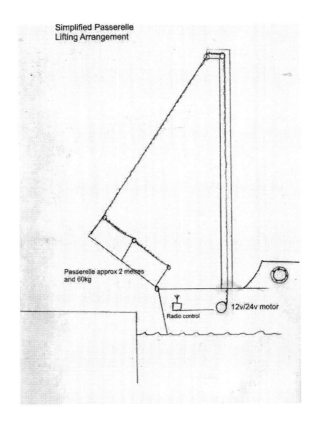

Simplified Passerelle
Lifting Arrangement

Passerelle approx 2 metres
and 60kg

Radio control

12v/24v motor

There you have it. A remotely controlled passerelle with all
the convenience and kudos of a super-yacht and a lot
quieter than hydraulic.

*Now the tricky bit I hinted at...

I found a problem on an early installation in that if the radio
receiver was placed too near the motor, it received
interference from the motor as it was lifting and that
stopped reception.

The result was that when the motor ran, it interfered with the
radio signal - then the motor would stop - then start again

15

as the radio unit kicked in because the motor was now in fact stopped and not interfering.

So, you ended up with the whole thing going into a - click-stop-click-stop-click-stop - sort of loop.

An easy remedy was to install the receiver as far away as one can, at least 2 metres if possible, from the motor.

Now let's talk about saving water ...

WATER SAVER

We all do it. We turn on the shower and run the water until it's hot, wasting water - depending on the pipe run. On my yacht with a long pipe run, about 3 litres of water per shower per person.

This reasonably economic system will save you precious water – particularly, as said, if you have a long pipe run from the boiler. It takes 40 seconds on my yacht for hot water to arrive in the aft heads - water that otherwise would be going down the drain into the waste tank or overboard.

In your installation check how much water is wasted by putting a bucket under the shower head and turn on the shower until running hot. Then check how many litres. (Or you can calculate the volume of cold water in the pipe - a 22mm pipe holds 0.320 litres per meter.)
That is valuable water that is wasted every time you take a shower.
On short runs it may not be worth the effort but on a long run it certainly is.

Let's analyse that waste. On my yacht say four people taking one shower each a day - that's (4x3) 12 litres a day wasted waiting for the water to run hot - 84 litres a week - and about 336 litres of good fresh water a month.

The principle is simple. At the press of a button in the bathroom (heads), an electric timer is set into motion. This opens a valve that diverts the hot water - which is not hot yet as it is further down the pipe - for the first x number of seconds. It is just returning cold water back to the tank.

The valve is timed to shut off when the hot water is at the shower mixer valve.

Following is the plan ...

Schematic: Water Saver

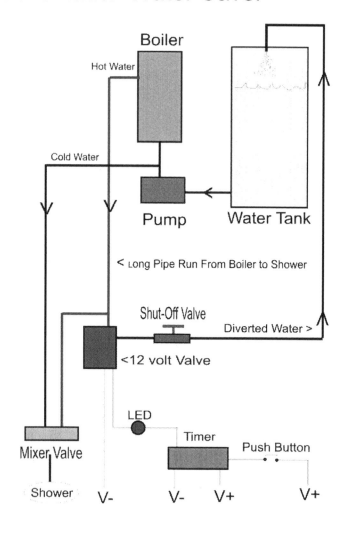

Set the timer for the time it takes the hot water to arrive at the shower mixer, that depends on the length of the pipe. As said my yacht is 53ft and has a pipe run to the aft cabin heads of about 9 metres - or about 40 seconds from the time the shower tap is turned on until hot water starts to flow.

The simplest and cheapest valves are 12-volt washing machine valves from, you guessed, eBay. One for each shower. If you only have 24 volts then the cheapest option is to install a 24-12 volt step down unit, starting from about £1 rather than trying to source 24-volt valves. Look at the end of the book for more details of these units.

12 volt Washing Machine Valve

You will need a timer, one for each shower - also via eBay at around €20 each.

Make up a simple panel with a push button and LED indicator light.

Now, procure enough tube to run from the closest point of the shower head back to the water tank and enough cable to connect your 12-volt supply to the timer, control switch and then to the water valves. Also, it is wise to install isolator valves - one before each washing machine valve, so that should they fail you can close the circuit.

I installed this system on my yacht about 7 years ago. It works brilliantly. Enter the bathroom. Press button on the water saver. Prepare for a shower. Hot water is almost instantly at the shower head by the time you are ready.
No waiting while watching cold water running from the shower and going overboard or into your waste tank and also, incidentally, cooling the shower room.

Work out how much water we have saved in 7 years with this?

WASTE PUMP BACKWASH

How often have you had to dismantle a filthy black/grey water tank pump because one of the valves had something stuck in it?

I installed this device a few years ago. When turned on it backwashes the pump(s) in seconds, clears the pipes and leaves the whole system filled with fresh, less corrosive, water - an added advantage if they do actually need servicing.

(1) You need enough pipe to run from a cold fresh-water point to your electric waste pump

(2) A lever operated ball valve

(3) A one-way valve - not necessary but my guests and crew feel happier when I explain how the system works.

Waste Pump Backwash

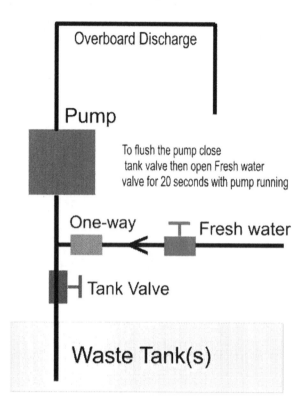

Overboard Discharge

Pump

To flush the pump close
tank valve then open Fresh water
valve for 20 seconds with pump running

One-way   Fresh water

Tank Valve

Waste Tank(s)

This is a shot of my installation.
I use two pumps in series as the tanks are quite big and the pumps also double up as bilge pumps so some complex plumbing but the principle is the same as the simplified diagram.

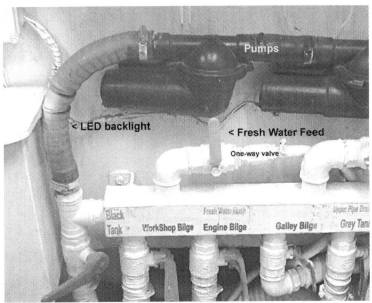

**The 'Pump-Out' arrangement on DriKé
showing the flushing valve (centre)**

So, if the pump is not priming because the valves are jammed with sludge - simply, while the pump is running - shut the valve to the tank at the same time open the fresh water valve. The pump will then prime almost immediately and wash all the gunge from the system. After about 10 - 20 seconds close the fresh water valve and re-open the tank valve. The pump and pipes are now primed full with fresh water and will start to pump immediately.

Another innovation I have used here is to insert a section of clear pipe on the intake side of the pump. Behind this pipe, I cable-clipped some LEDs wired into the pump circuit. I can now see if the pipes are primed or when pumping has stopped.

Note: As said above the one-way valve is not necessary. The manifold is under vacuum - it is sucking. The water is under pressure. There is no way that the waste tank can run into the freshwater system.

The valve is there so I can point it out to curious guests and crew that this is an extra security feature for their peace of mind.

EASILY CONVERT YOUR EXISTING MANUAL TOILET TO AN ALL-ELECTRIC LUXURY SYSTEM

Convert your existing manual toilet into a freshwater electric system using simple and relatively cheap components.

On my yacht I had three toilet compartments - now two as I since commandeered one for use as a super utility cupboard ... just bragging.

The remaining two toilets units were, in my opinion, the worst design of a toilet ever created - and certainly not by someone who lives onboard.

They were Blake's Lavac's!
Nasty, horrible things.
They should be illegal!!!

It was very touching optimism on part of the manufacturers that when you finished using the loo you closed the lid that was supposed to form an air-tight seal. Then vigorously work the hand pump with the belief, the faith, that seawater would enter and the waste would go out.

You then waited until the vacuum thus created equalised so you could lift the lid for final inspection and see that the toilet was empty and in pristine condition. Except it does not work like that!

The lid often did not seal and if it did there was often an occurrence were the vacuum and vigorous pumping turned the contents of the bowl into what looked like a frothy mulligatawny soup. - absolutely revolting!

My wife screamed when she once used the toilet after me and it had not flushed properly.

Often if the user tried to lift the lid while still under vacuum the lid would crack (I have seen this on other boats). Thus, not allowing a full vacuum to be created requiring you to purchase new lid/seat. Now, another joke from this company, a replacement seat/lid, and a seal only cost a whopping £180.00 – just a toilet seat and a rubber ring! Shame on them.

So, let's start and make a super, all electric, loo.

For each toilet obtain the now ubiquitous 12-volt washing machine valve (around €6) (The same type as the water saver) and a macerator pump. Jabsco are very good, albeit expensive. €150-€180 or more. So also look at Surgeflo pumps on eBay or direct from www.unifloproducts.co.uk.

They look like a clone of the Jabsco and are far cheaper and you CAN easily get spare parts from their website

You need a pipe from a cold-water supply and a power supply to the pump.

Now I choose to flush the toilets with fresh water for several reasons:

(1) You will already have pressurised cold water feed in the heads

(2) Freshwater does not cause the same awful smell as saltwater.

(3) I am much happier with fresh water going into my steel tanks rather than sea water.

(4) There is far less calcium build-up in the pipes.

(5) Waste pumps and diaphragms will last longer handling fresh water.

(6) One more seacock can be removed - one less hole in the bottom of your hull.

[In fact, you will use very little fresh water, easily compensated for if you install the water saver as I detailed earlier in this book.]

To continue: you can use either a two-way centre return none-latching switch or two push buttons to control the water in - waste out. I also suggest a relay to run the pump. Pumps are an inductive load and use a whack of power when starting so a 30-amp relay is a good idea to take the load off the switch.

Fill - Empty Control Panel

It was very simple to convert the original toilets from frothy, smelly things to super cool units good enough to garner favourable comments from my guests - especially if they were also used to using Blakes Lavacs.

A note: As we are liveaboards the toilet pumps gets a lot of use. I always keep (several) spare pumps ready to re-fit.

These pumps do not need to be bolted to a bulkhead – no point, they are not going anywhere - and that just increases the noise through transmitted vibration and takes much longer to remove. Mine are suspended on a short, thick piece of bungee cord that hangs from a hook. The electrical connections are push fit 15 amp of the lucar type.

Spare pump in waiting

I have been timed: to replace a blocked or faulty macerator pump...starting now!

(1) Shut off the input valve - see below *

(2) Gently pull out the electrical connections

28

(3) Remove two hose clips (I have a small socket/ratchet set ready for this.)

(4) Un-hook the bungee and remove the pump.

Reverse procedure to refit the spare - total time of three minutes.

Input Valve

Another innovation I recommend it to fit a 1¼" shut-off valve as close to the pump as possible on the toilet side - the reason is that if/when the pump becomes blocked or becomes faulty then that section of pipe can be isolated. As it would probably be still full of excrement this prevents the contents of the pipe draining into the bilges and over your hands when you remove the pump.

It is indeed horrible without one!

FITTING A RADIO CONTROL TO YOUR BOW THRUSTER

Advice and tips on the correct units to buy
and how to install them

Have you had this scenario?

You have just one crew and she/he is at the stern handling the lines. You are heading to the bow to attach the lazy line or throw a line to the jetty. There is now no one is at the helm (where the bow thruster controls are.)

A gust of wind and the bow starts to pay off and you are a long way from the helm. No problem, you have a remote control on a lanyard around your neck.
 A couple of deft touches and the bow returns back to place like a well-trained sheepdog. No fuss, no shouting.

They are so cheap to buy and simple to install - I don't know why more people don't fit them.

I covered the types of radio controls in the chapter on the lifting passerelle but will copy the same information again to save you flipping back through the pages.

You will note these come in two major frequencies - 433MHz and 315MHz. They are not interchangeable. Technically 315Mhz is not allowed in Europe, while both 315Mhz and 433Mhz are allowed in the USA so 433Mhz would be a better choice as simply put politically - worldwide frequency that can be used everywhere. It depends on what is available and at what price.

Also, 433 MHz is supposed to have a longer range than 315 MHz although I have not noticed this in practice - I think it depends more on the quality of the unit itself.

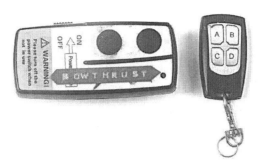

Typical Radio Control Fobs

Four channel receiver

You also need to make sure the model you buy is of the correct type - you will need one that has 'momentary contact' not 'latching'. Some on the market have the ability to change this arrangement with 'jumpers' (small tabs to connect or disconnect parts of the circuit.)

If you are worried about buying the correct one visit my website www.ChrisSouthwood.com - then scroll to boats and look at the submenu for 'Electric Passerelle Bits'.
(I plan to 'drop ship' these items later in the year. Sure, you could buy cheaper direct but I will get you the correct one.)

Wiring should be simple. Find just two wires that connect positive to the thruster solenoid and the one used for negative and wire in parallel.

Install a safety switch and a LED indicator into the circuit or preferably a key switch so that it cannot be accidentally turned on - it also looks cool.

The same applies to adding a remote control to an electric anchor winch.

You may note that the radio units I suggest are mostly four channels so you could use just one unit to operate both the bow-thruster and the anchor. I don't really recommend this because the buttons are a bit close together. You could, by mistake, operate the anchor instead of the bow-thrusters and look a bit of a Charlie.
Besides they are cheap enough to buy so it is best to have two units and keep them separate on coloured lanyards and just take on deck the one you need.

IF YOUR MAIN BATTERY SUPPLY IS 24 VOLTS
DO YOU REALY NEED A SEPARATE 12-VOLT BATTERY BANK?

For a long time I maintained a brace of 12 volt batteries wired in parallel to supply the current to power things like the VHF, stereo, instruments, charging sockets for phones and so on.

On my yacht, the only way I could charge the 12-volt bank of batteries was by running the generator with the output split by a diode between generator start and 12volt service batteries.
Not very efficient because when running only on the main engine there was no way I could charge the 12-volt side of things.

Eventually as the batteries aged, they needed replacing – as batteries do.

So, some thought, then an idea, then a solution that has worked brilliantly

So, the idea.
How much energy did I need for the 12volt side of things? A simple calculation and with all loads running (with the exception of the VHF on transmit), was a maximum of around 4 amp. So why not do away with the 12 volts batteries altogether, save space, cost and weight? And instead use a modern 24 to 12 volt drop down converter?
At around €15 euros, as against about €150 for new batteries, it was worth trying.

So duly ordered and installed with a circuit breaker from the 24-volt side and a fuse on the 12-volt side.

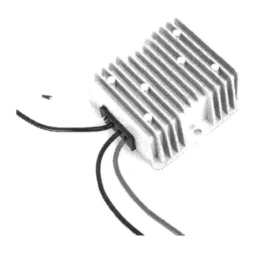

My initial worry was how hot, i.e. how efficient this unit would be, and how much electrical noise that may be picked up by any audible devices such as the stereos and VHF?

No worries. The unit does not even get warm, and there is no discernible noise.

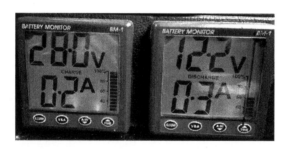

I rewired my existing Nasa volt/amp metre. The 24-volt battery is on the left and shows a float charge.

The 12-volt on the right shows a steady 12.2 volts output and the amperage obviously depending on load. The battery capacity monitor on the 12-volt gauge is obviously redundant.

I opted for a 30-amp converter in order to cater for any conceivable load – a bit overkill, I could have used a smaller one, but seems efficient and the price at around €15 was not an issue. (Also ordered a spare)

Alternatives.

This may not suit everybody or every installation.

However, there will always be situation when, for example, you don't want to run a new cable from your 12-volt bank just for a cabin light or new gadget. No problem.

Individual converters are on the market for very little money.
This is the first example for light loads
The MM2596 Buck Converter

. These start at about €1.50 and will handle up to around 3 amps. Search for something similar to this:
'*DC-DC Boost Buck adjustable step up down Converter*'

The small screw at the lower middle left adjusts the voltage output.

Input voltage 4.5 volts to 40 volts, Adjustable output voltage below the input voltage is 1.5volt to 35 volts. Max load 2 amps or 3 amps with a heat-sink. Conversion efficiency is around 92% (The higher the output voltage the greater the efficiency.)

Moving up to higher power handling the next one example is rated at 5 amp and costs around €8.50

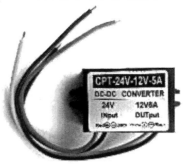

Search for something like this:
DC 24V to 12V 5A 60W Buck Converter Step-Down Car Power Supply Voltage Regulator

Just a couple of ways to get 12-volt without additional wiring. All available on eBay, most from China, mostly free postage and all take about 2-5 weeks to arrive.

HIGH BILGE-WATER & EXCESSIVE PUMP ACTIVITY ALARM

It is always good to know if there is an unusual amount of water entering your boat - sort of essential if you want to stay afloat.

I had a situation where a 35mm pipe had become unattached and was back siphoning into the boat and I had no warning that this was happening. The bilge pump in that section was not coping with that amount of water. Luckily, I found out when the water hit the electric boiler and the shore power tripped. If I had been off the boat at the time it could have been very serious - offending pipe now re-plumbed.

So, I decided to install an alarm system. Separate float switches to monitor high bilge water and trigger an alarm can be expensive particularly if you have several separate bilge water collection points. Also double the amount of float switches equals double the maintenance.

On my yacht I have three such areas; forward cabins, engine room and workshop, where the stern-tube lives (The rear cabin area and rudder stock, drains into the workshop sump.)

At first, I experimented by fitting a buzzer in parallel with the bilge pump lights so I had an audible alarm when the pump is running. I added a diode in each pump circuit as one does not want to energise all the pumps if only one pump runs. (I could have installed a separate buzzer for each pump but diodes are simpler and cheaper.)

Sounds good except if you have a regular drip from the stern tube, as normal, you do not want to be woken at three in the morning by the alarm when the pump only wants to run for about 10 seconds.

The ideal would be to set up a system whereby the pumps deal with their normal business; that is, they are only running for 10 - 20 seconds at a time and they do not need to set off an alarm. However, if they are still pumping after a minute (or whatever time you adjust it to) then something may be wrong and worth checking.

This is how it works with a delay, for illustration purposes, set for one minute;

When the pump first kicks in via the float-switch the timer is set in motion. The first switch in series is the normally closed relay on the timer itself and that is now open so no current flows to the alarm.

Simultaneously an ancillary normally open relay, also wired in series in the pump circuit, is energised and is in the closed position.

For one minute the timer contact is open and the ancillary relay closed - no current is flowing to the alarm.

After a minute the timer will switch off and its relay will go to the normally closed position.

However, if the pump is still running then we have the ancillary relay still energised and is thus in the on position, both contacts, timer and ancillary relay, are in continuity, IE they are on, and the alarm will then sound.

(Remember, you will need to install diodes to prevent the pump that is running feeding power to the other pumps.)

Bilge Pump Alarm

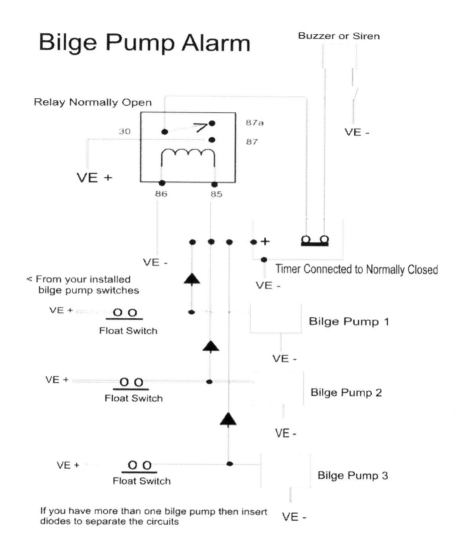

So instead of having to buy, say, three float-switches, cable and buzzers plus a lot of work to install, you have with the above a system that allows you to sleep and warns you of excessive pump activity long before the water level gets too high.

You will need a timer (eBay) a buzzer and some diodes and the whole thing can be installed in about an hour.

This is a typical timer that can be found on eBay.

For this project set the jumpers to OP1. The timing adjuster is on minimum when turned fully clockwise. Obviously, these timers will vary depending on the make.

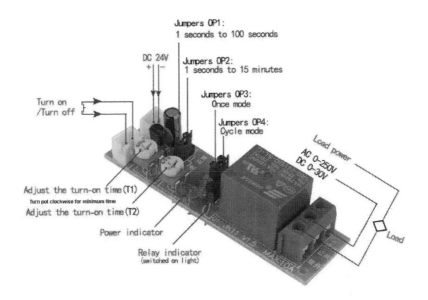

GAS OR ELECTRIC?
How to Install an All-Electric Galley

Most yachts have gas cookers as the primary method of cooking. Why?

I considered this from all aspects and came to the following conclusions:

Why gas? look at the problems and dangers of gas, either butane or propane - both are known as 'LPG' or Liquefied Petroleum Gas,

1. LPG is dangerous. We all know that it is heavier than air and any leak will accumulate in the bilges. If not well ventilated it becomes a waiting bomb. Look at http://bit.do/Gas-Explosion This is a short video by Yachting Monthly of an average boat blowing up with a butane gas cylinder – bit scary.

2. Gas cooking is by naked flame, greatly increasing the risk of fire if a pan with oil should overheat

3. Gas cookers are heavy and difficult to clean particularly when gimballed allowing bits of food or splashes to fall down the sides and back.

4. The smell of bottled gas is unpleasant

5. Even when things are running correctly complete combustion results in the formation of carbon dioxide and water vapour. Neither are wanted. But worse still, carbon monoxide is a by-product of combustion when there is not

42

enough oxygen to burn the LPG completely. i.e. you could be adding a dangerous amount of carbon dioxide/monoxide into your boat particularly if ventilation sources are inadequate – such as in winter when hatches and vents are closed, that can be, and often is, lethal.

Leaking or un-burnt LPG stops your body's ability to absorb oxygen often leading to crew complaining of feeling drowsy similar to the effects of a hangover when using propane gas cookers.

Remember, for every kilo of gas burnt a kilo of liquid is also vented into your boat causing corrosion, mildew and respiratory problem.

6. Of course, one should fit gas, CO/CO2 monitors and alarms. These will minimise the risks - but not eliminate them.

7. Gas cylinders are not easily interchangeable when sailing from one country or region to another.

8. Gas is no longer as cheap as it used to be. Price of a gas refill seems to ignore the base price of oil and have increased out of proportion.

9. Refilled gas bottles can be hard to find when cruising plus when you do find a shop that has them in stock, they are heavy to carry back to your boat. You are not allowed to take them onto a bus.

10. A dedicated locker or storage area is required to house the gas bottles – you will need more than one bottle – and they always seem to run out just when you are cooking a complex meal – so that involves scrabbling in the gas locker with a torch changing over bottles or valves.

Of course, not all boats (or owners) are set up to make an all-electric galley possible – but read on.

About a year before I completely changed over to an all-electric galley, I bought a single free-standing induction hob, an Oibrgozo PI4800, from Carrefour for €38. This could be set from 400 to 2,000 watts when cooking. It was brilliant, perhaps three times faster than my gas cooker to bring a pot to the boil. And the advertising claims induction is 55% quicker and more efficient than other electric hobs.

Also being made from one piece of glass makes it so easy to clean. The glass does not get very hot; induction cooking heats only the steel in the base of the pan*, so spilt food does not bake onto the surface – and the other plus is that my marina has a fixed price for electricity – so basically no extra running cost. (Induction hobs are very efficient so you will cook in far less time than conventional systems)

*You will have to check that your pans are suitable for induction cooking – is should tell you on the bottom of the pan.

My old Plastimo propane cooker was awful; why they are called 'marine' cookers when so much of it is made of cheap mild steel (The plastic knobs fell off in the first year because they were held on by mild steel clips that rusted away.) The grill was positioned so that oil and fats from anything cooking on the hobs fell on it so when you lit the grill the accumulated grease had to burn off filling the galley with smoke. The oven was incredibly slow and hard to light – and this cost me €800 15 years ago.

A year earlier I bought a simple three element electric cooker as it was far faster than the microwave and maybe five times faster than the Calor gas oven. For example, I can grill a pizza, piping hot and crusty, in less than ten minutes.

I was also using a microwave – so, why did I still have gas? Good question.

I jotted down some figures:
Selling the original gas cooker and getting some money back on the cylinders bought in over €250. I bought another single induction hob. As they are two separate units, I have redundancy and will still have one functioning unit should one fail. (Plus, I already had the single hob unit from the year before).

I now have two hobs totally separate for the cost of €76.00 I also decided to up-grade the electric cooker to a 22-litre version for the cost of €80.00

Fitting the hobs took a little bit of cunning as they were originally designed to sit on the counter top. It was worth the extra work to recess them so they were completely flush. Checking of course they still had adequate ventilation.

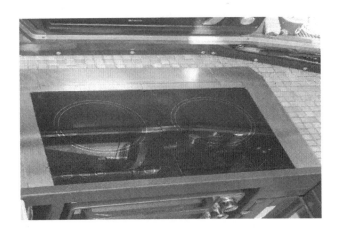

Now, the disadvantages:

Obviously, power. If you are in a marina then you need to keep your amperage to withing the working tolerances of the shore supply. If you have space heaters, battery chargers, twin hobs, oven, washing machine and microwave you need to be selective with what you are using.

I have fitted a very useful meter in the galley that shows volts and amps – fairly essential actually.

Away from the marina you will need a generator of at least 4kw. I found when cruising I had to run the generator anyway to charge the batteries and produce hot water when the engine was not running. Also arrange to have the generator controls, stop/start in the galley so the chef can easily operate as required.

Ah, you say "What if the generator malfunctions while cruising, how do you cook are heat your food?"
Then for peace of mind fit an inverter of at least two kilowatts – obviously the bigger the better. but the price goes up exponentially. A two-kilowatt pure sine wave

inverter* will cost about €120. A four kilowatt about €350 – but shop around and make sure, doubly sure, that the wattage is the 'constant' rate, not the 'peak' rate.

An alternative is to buy two x 2-kilowatt units (again redundancy if one should fail) and wire these separately to each unit. (Plus, some ingenuity with changeover switches.) In use you may need to keep the engine running to feed these as they will be heavy on amperage.

* While researching I read in yachting forums about whether a square wave form inverter (the cheaper type) will power an induction hob. The answer seems to be "It depends on the inverter and it depends on the hob!". My advice is to go for a 'pure sine wave inverter' to be sure it will function.
You can of course use the inverter for say, boiling the kettle, without having to start the generator – depending on your battery capacity.
And if you do want to slow cook a romantic evening meal without the generator running induction hobs are very efficient. You can simmer at just 400 watts to prepare a meal with a lid on the pan. No gas smell and a greasy cooker to clean.

Of course, the perfect solution would be to have enough solar panels to provide all the power for cooking. Free, no pollution, no noise ... well, one day.
I now have an all-electric galley. The induction hobs are fantastic, quick and easy to clean. The whole arrangement is safer with no gas fumes or naked flames.

The new, all electric galley on my yacht, DriKe

I have reduced the overall weight of the cooking equipment by 25killos (not important on my boat, but on a smaller boat that is an appreciable saving. And I now have the full use of a locker where the gas bottles used to live.

Ahh! You will may say "How do you stop the pans sliding of the glass hobs while sailing?"

This is easily accomplished by a cunning piece of plywood with holes cut for the largest pan – you should always use your larger pans when heeling and no more than 1/3rd full. To each cut-out, at around 120 degree intervals, bolt with wing nuts three 40mm wooden disks (easily cut from scrap wood with disk cutter) and mount these off-centre so that when they are turned they close the gap on the smaller pans.

Stows away when not in use and simply clips in place when needed. (Although I personally have never cooked when the boat is on its ear in a force 9. Far too unpleasant. Pre-prepared Sandwiches and cuppa-soups are adequate.)

{And no worries about the heat. An induction hob only heats the steel in the base of the pan. The hob gets warm by the heat reflected from the pan, and does not get hot enough to damage the plywood – particularly as it is not actually in the induction areas.}

.

WATER LEVEL INDICATOR FOR ABOUT €3.50

This very cheap and simple to construct device can be used anywhere you need to monitor fluid levels: Bilges, holding tanks, water tanks - etc.

I am still experimenting with this but let me share what I have learnt and done so far. This is the basic wiring diagram

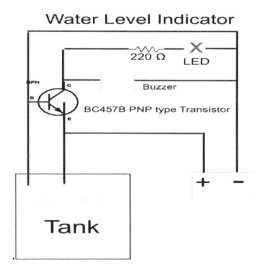

The principle is very simple. Two sensors (or one if the tank is steel and is used as the ground electrode) will trigger a relay, buzzer or led when both electrodes are immersed and the circuit is completed.

This will not show you the gradient content but will trigger, say, when the tank is full, or a second or third electrode will trigger when half, three-quarters full and so on.

The only problem, so far, is that the sensor(s) need to be kept clean else if they stay 'wet' through accumulated surface dirt the system will still be in an alarm state when the fluid level drops. I am experimenting with a different electrode material.

So have a look, try it out.... on future updates to this book I will let you know how these are working including wiring via a relay to make a solid-state float-switch for the bilges.

(Have you experienced how incredibly unreliable and expensive of-the-shelf float switches from you are? If you have owned a boat for a few years you will know)

CUSTOM MADE LED LIGHT FITTINGS

Some led bulbs are expensive, you can easily be charged €50 plus for an anchor light. No more said - make your own Led light fitting very cheaply and easily.

Let's start with just two examples using led strip lights that that can be bought on eBay for about €5. Led strip is the most versatile and with a bit of ingenuity almost any bulb or fitting can be fabricated

Buy a roll of led strip light on eBay. These come in several types. Waterproof has a silicone type material to protect the copper. Non-waterproof has a coating of what looks like shellac - both need careful preparation when soldering the wire tails - see below.

When choosing led strips - usually on a coil - look at the number of LEDs, hence brightness, per metre. For example, 30 or 60 LEDs per metre are typical and note that they come in all colours - warm white is best for general lighting. Try to avoid cold white - they make people look like zombies.

A candlestick light

Cut a piece of dowel about 40 mm in length. Drill two 2mm holes in the base the same width as the existing socket and insert two panel pins. Cut a section of led strip and solder on two wire tails. Apply a thin coat of contact adhesive to the dowel. Wrap the led strip around the dowel and solder the wire tails to the pins - finished.

I have made my own navigation lights using this idea - yes, sure, I accept they will not pass coastguard regulations in various countries but they are bright and easily made. Say these are for temporary use until you can buy the genuine and approved article when the light-bulb inspectors arrive - that said the ones on DriKé are now in their fifth year.

(Off the shelf navigation lights cost in the region of €25. Home-made cost about €1 and they appear as bright.)

Reading Light

Rather than trying to make a bulb that plugs into the centre cut your led strip and using contact adhesive wrap around the inside rim of the lamp. Works well with a better light distribution.

If you have a 24-volt system you can still use 12 volts led strips - just divide the circuit into two equal sections and wire in series.

Some Soldering Notes

It takes a little bit of skill and practise when connecting the wire tails.

This is how.

You will need a fine soldering iron - or wrap some 2.5 mm copper wire around the tip of the soldering iron leaving about 25mm at the tip.

After you cut the required section - they have indicators where to cut - typically at intervals of three LEDs apart either 25mm, 50mm or 100mm.

You need to very carefully remove the silicone or shellac covering with a scalpel or similar small sharp knife to get to the copper connectors. Then clean these with very fine glass paper.

Holding the soldering iron like a pen push down firmly into the cleaned copper contact and then apply just enough solder to, as quickly as possible, 'tin' the copper. It is important it does not get too hot. Similarly, tin the wire tails Then when bringing together it just needs a touch of about one second to complete the connection.

Use wire as thin as possible to save putting too much mechanical pressure on the joint or needing excessive heat to melt the solder.

Also, note that led strip is polarity conscious - the positive is marked throughout the strip but not always the negative.

VIDEO MONITOR

Something else I added for very little money that you may be interested in is a closed-circuit video monitor.

These, in fact, are car reversing cameras and cost around €20-€40 for the complete kit. You could install these to monitor all areas of your boat and/or engine room - most have two channels.

I installed one in my forward cabin before a hip operation because I knew I would be very immobile. Without moving, I could see who was calling around (I also installed a remote radio doorbell hung from the passerelle.)

So - provided I actually wanted to welcome them when they called - I could lower the passerelle, also by radio remote, without moving to let them on board.

Simple to install - no plan necessary. Search on eBay with the search criteria *Car Reversing Camera.*

BOW THRUSTER BATTERIES

"Yes, I know. I should have a fuse or a breaker in series with my bow-thruster batteries!"
'The battery lament' © Chris Southwood 2018

My yacht is 53ft, weighs 35 tonnes, and has an unbalanced rudder the size of a door that locks over and without the bow-thruster makes steering astern almost impossible.
I did once have a fuse but the silly, petulant, thing would blow just when I really needed one more blast to avoid my neighbour's small biscuit thin plastic boat when manoeuvring astern into my berth against a strong crosswind. So, I removed it - the fuse that is.

As a 'fun' video of the horrid spectre of being committed to reversing one kilometre with only a bow-thruster for steering, search YouTube with this phrase:

Navigating the Canal Entrance to the Mar-Menor as the Bridge is Closing....'

The scene opens as a cruising companion on another yacht was overtaking me in the canal entrance to get to the lifting bridge before it, as he erroneously thought, would be closing for the rest of the afternoon.

What he had not noticed, because of his low-slung bimini, (in fact it was an almost collapsing bimini and looked more like a Bedouin tent and was obstructing the view up and ahead), was that the bridge had already closed - an

58

ambulance on an emergency call needed to cross and it, naturally, had priority!

He hit the bridge and was stuck tight against the parapet by the current with his mast tangled in the pedestrian handrails. I was behind him.

You can see me commencing a long reverse up the canal that was too narrow to turn around in - plus there was an appreciable current running. I was praying that the fuse would not overheat and blow as I was single handed and the bow thruster was my only means of steering.

Yes, I know. Tell me again - I should have a fuse or a trip in circuit with my bow-thruster batteries! I am not advising you to remove yours, because a few months ago when returning against a strong side wind I had to give the thruster a lot of 'wellie'. I did notice, almost subliminally, the smell of battery acid but did not check. A day later, there was a huge bang!

One of the thruster batteries had been cooking overnight and had – literally- blown up!

Solution - with or without fuse or breaker - is as follows;
buy, again on eBay, a temperature sensor with alarm and
relay output, should cost around €6-€10.
Search for something like;

*Digital LED Temperature Controller Switch Thermostat Control
Switch.*

Simply attach with a cable-tie the probe so that it is in
physical contact with the battery terminal.
Make sure you have a buzzer or siren loud enough to be
heard in any part of the boat and wire this in series with the
relay on the controller.
Add a 'kill switch' to prevent your crew panicking if the
system is triggered - you can see mine to the left of the
panel.
Set the alarm for, say, 40c but you can experiment with that.

Here you see my setup. The battery is ambient at 28.3c with
the alarm set for 40c. Just keep an eye on that when coming
in astern using the thruster.

You could of course invest in a few of these units and
install in various parts of your boat - engine room, battery
compartments, generator housing etc.

I also advise installing smoke detectors as an addition in vulnerable locations particularly where you may have a lot of heavy wiring - near the anchor windless or bow-thruster for example. A loose or corroded connection pulling about 500 amps can get very hot. I have seen one such installation set fire and burn through a wooden bulkhead - all due to a loose nut.

No comment or comparison please.

SEAGULL POO, TEAK DECKS & A GRUMPY SKIPPER

A short time ago I moved my yacht to the far end of my jetty. It was much quieter there plus a better view of the sunsets.
But there was a problem - seagulls also prefer the top end of the jetty and they feel it is really cool to land on my mast-head or spreaders and deliberately dump gallons of guano all over my deck - and sometimes down my open hatches.

These guys must eat some interesting stuff to produce such quantities of revolting mess that looks like someone has chucked a bucket of lumpy white-wash on my lovely teak.

First thing I did, as one does, was to look on the internet for some form of bird repellent. Favourite (for the seller) seemed to be some rather expensive owl cut-outs or shiny disks you hang from string - all plus tax and P&P

I tried several ideas. Now the first one is not by any means a new idea, nor is it an original, so apologies if you have heard of this before - but it works.

On my yacht I loosely strung together with cable ties some old CD's - dull side together with the shiny side out. I made up just two of these units and hoisted them on my flag halyard as far as the first spreader.
Now the purpose of tying them loosely is so they wobble in the slightest breeze. Birds seem frightened by flashing lights and they stay away. This arrangement was effective even

though the first spreader is some way from the top of the mast where the gulls mostly landed.

So far - so good. Two weeks now and no need to clean the decks almost every day as I had before.

Another idea that I have tried is a 'hawk' cut-out using a piece of aluminium. This tends to put them off.

An amusing story to go with this section on Seagulls:

These devices seem to keep seagulls away from my boat. However, for a short period I was rafted up to a rather scruffy boat in the marina. The owner was hardly ever there. The problem with his boat is that the top of his masts (a ketch) were flat – perfect landing places for seagulls.

As they took off, they pooped, dumping their 'cargo', that looked like buckets of whitewash. As the wind is mostly westerly in this marina, and I was to the east, it landed downwind all over my teak decks.

So, whenever I saw a seagull land on the mast I leant over with a boathook and banged on his rigging to frighten them away.
On one particular day I saw one land on his mizzen mast. I grabbed the boat hook and banged frantically on the rigging - I remember shouting wildly something like "Stop s####ing on my decks!!!".

There was a female scream from my neighbour's boat - they had returned unbeknown to me - the owner came rushing up from down below with a terrified look on his face.

Many profuse apologies were given and a wimpish wave of my hand to point out the distressing state of my decks.

A week later I moved further down the jetty, to me and my neighbour's relief - and the seagulls could now go about their business with impunity.

My own gull deterrents were still in place, and still work. No bother since then.

64

Ok, Toots, I know when I am not wanted,
I'll find another boat.

FENDER SENSE

Always make sure you have enough fenders.

So now we talk about fenders, super! Seriously, a few tips.

If you moor in a marina one of the annoying things after a blow is to find some of your fenders have gone missing. Most yachtsmen's, being nice honest chaps, when they find a lost item will attempt to return it to the rightful owner – if they know which boat it belongs to that is.

Solution: take a soldering iron and 'brand' the name of the boat, or its initials in the thick piece of plastic at the top of the fender. Then, hopefully, when you lose a fender and it happily bobs to the other side of the dock it will be retrieved by an equally happy sailor who thought they had a free fender but, on seeing the name, happiness rapidly abated, will make the effort to find you and return it. It could also prevent squabbles when tied alongside another boat when the time to cast off and sort fenders comes.

Don't hang your fenders upside-down.

Fenders have a small valve, usually brass or stainless, in the body of the fender in order to inflate them.

Most people don't know this - they should, for safety, always be hung so this valve is pointing towards the water. The reason is if you hit the dock a bit too hard and one of your crew is at the side helping to fend off, as good crew do, then if the fender is crushed the valve may shoot out with quite some force.

If your crew is looking at the fender then the valve could hit them in the eye like a bullet – so, always: valve side down.

My marina is blasted by sand from the beach during high winds. So regularly wash your fenders to remove sticky particles of sand that would act, literally like sand paper and will rapidly scour your, and your neighbours' topsides if you are squashed together.

Let them see you doing this, tell them why, and you will probably be invited for a beer or two.

EVER-LASTING FLAGS

Totally fed-up having to replace my Spanish courtesy flag after every blow I came up with a simple solution – make one from aluminium.

Check on the internet the exact proportions – for example the Spanish flag follows the traditional 2:3 ratio.

A horizontal tricolour of red, yellow (double width) and red; charged with the Spanish coat of arms off-centred toward the hoist.
(I have left the coat of arms off as these as I don't believe these are required on a courtesy flag, however if you feel artistic you can add these).

So, two horizontal stripes of red (top and bottom) and yellow (middle). The yellow stripe is twice the size of the red stripes.

Ready to hoist

WELDING PLASTIC.

Plastic is great. Plastic breaks. Plastic can be expensive to replace if they are part of a 'marine' bit of kit. From a computer case to a water tank there is a simple way to make a welded repair.

Tools: ideal are one of those miniature blow-lamps that are becoming readily available. Failing that a soldering iron.

You will need a few mixed cable ties – available in all sorts of colours to match the item for repair.

The technique is to very gently apply local heat the plastic until it just starts to melt – then introduce the cable ties at about the same angle you

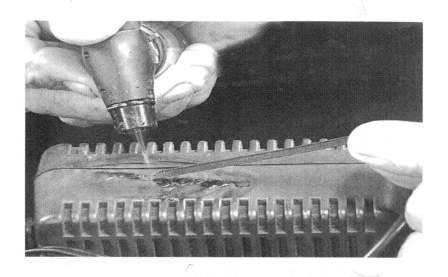

would hold a pen.
Slowly fill the break or crack with the plastic 'weld'. Job finished.

To improve the appearance of the work you can smooth down the repair with a bit if wet/dry paper.

I have repaired all sorts if broken plastic this way. If you are lucky enough to have plastic from the same item then even better as plastics vary enormously and the ideal would be to have a section of plastic from same batch.

A few More Hints and Tips *HILIGHT*
I thought I would finish this book with a few more thoughts on boaty bits.

Sharp Edges.

One thing that stood out, literately, when I first bought my yacht was the number of right-angled edges in the joinery work though-out the boat.
Super fun if you are thrown against them in rough weather. Rib cracking fun in fact.

So, if your boat has similar sharp bits take a few hours rounding off the edges. If the edge is plywood and not solid wood this can be dealt with either by applying some veneer or by dipping your finger in some brown paint and rubbing into the exposed, finely sanded, plywood edge - it is surprising how good this looks.

SHARP EDGES ON CABLE TIES

A simple tip that prevents scratches and sometimes deep cuts:
Cable ties are great for keeping wires and tubing neat on board.
A problem though is when the surplus is trimmed this leaves a sharp edge that can lead to cuts when working close and brushing past the wiring loom – usually when upside down in the bilges.

The remedy is simple - after trimming the cable tie run a hot air gun, cigarette lighter or even a match over the cut end to slightly melt, and thus smooth, the sharp plastic– no more cuts, blood and bad language.

PAINTING

When varnishing or painting between coats rather than returning your brush to the jar of dissolvent tightly wrap the brush with aluminium foil. The paint stays wet on the brush for up to a day and is ready to use immediately on the next coat rather than having to dry out the brush.

Also, when you do put your brush back into the jar of dissolvent drill a hole in the handle so that when you push a bit of wire through the hole the base of the brush is suspended about 25mm above the bottom of the jar where all the crud forms. The old paint gently falls away so when needed again the brush is pretty smart.

When you need to re-touch a small area of paint - say a small scratch - rather than having to use a brush and cleaning it again do the job with a cotton bud from your medicine cupboard. Saves a lot of dissolvent and mess.

PREPARING STEEL & HAVING HAPPY NEIGHBOURS.

If you have a steel boat or need to work on other steel bits the best way to remove the inevitable rust is with an angle grinder - unfortunately this also fills the air with fine steel particles that settle like snow on both your, and your neighbours boat and starts rusting within a few hours leaving very hard to remove rust spots. Oxalic acid is good for removing stains but the effect on fine steel particles is it only takes off the first few microns of rust - but that still leaves the steel particle to continue rusting! The only way to remove this is a fairly abrasive scouring pad - not a happy situation and it does cause grumpy neighbours. So, don't use an angle grinder in the harbour or near other boats particularly in a strong wind.

A needle gun is very good for removing rust but they do require a powerful compressor and the noise is just this side of insanity.

If you don't have a needle gun and absent neighbours then to remove rust effectively without filling the air with steel try using a masonry bit with your drill set to 'hammer' mode. Still noisy, but less than a needle gun, however, respect your neighbours and work a bit at a time - say 20 minutes on each job rather than a whole morning or day, especially when they are doing yoga meditation on deck.

When using keep the bit about 30 degrees to the work and use firm pressure. The rust is removed fairly quickly and in much larger particles than an angle grinder so they do not become air-born. The finish is shiny and pitted. Clean with acetone or a preparatory de-greaser. This leaves an ideal key for the first coat of primer. And your neighbours will still like you...

Of course, for larger jobs take your boat to the boatyard and rig up a tarpaulin, or as I have done, take her to sea and use the generator to power the angle grinder - plus a powerful vacuum cleaner to collect the particles as soon as possible after the work and before they get damp.
Of course, if you have a fibreglass boat and your neighbour has a steel boat show them this article - a sort of hint on how to behave.
Speaking of oxalic or phosphoric acid there are dozens of propriety products that are based on these compounds.

A segue into the quaint notion that anything to do with boats must garner higher prices. The marine industry will not let you down on that score and will charge you a very hefty wedge for their products because it has 'boat/marine/yacht' on the label albeit it can be a quarter the price in other markets.
Search around. If you can get hold of a tub of this stuff you can make up a litre of this for cents rather than about €10, for example, that 'Ferronet' costs - that's the pinkish stuff in a plastic bottle that is sold to remove rust stains without telling you what it actually contains.

Here in Spain, I have bought very cheaply a product sold to clean paella pans called *'Limpiador de Cacerolas Paellas y Olla*'s this is from my local supermarket, Mercadona, and costs about €1.50 rather than €10. Whatever part of the world you live try shopping around - you will find an equivalent.

Another product that is used to protect steel is pure phosphoric acid - sometimes called 'Navel Gel'. This is a milky substance that is painted on rusty steel and converts rust from iron oxide to iron phosphate. As you paint it on it almost miraculously turns the rust into a hard, shiny black finish.

Trouble is it does not last. It becomes hygroscopic, that is it starts to absorb water. After about 18 months the rust reappears under the coating and the originally hard finish has now turned soft.

It does have a use if you clean the steel to remove as much rust as possible. (Slopping it on to a badly rusted and pitted surface, alas, as said, it looks good at first, but it does not last.)

After you get a shiny surface with just a few pit-marks degrease with acetone or similar. Then apply the acid. As said, it's like milk in density so easy to work.

As it is water-based wait until it is properly dry and hardened then wash with soapy water or degreaser to remove any acid that has not converted otherwise the 'loose' acid will attract water under the paint and continue the rusting process.

You should end up with a finish where the rust has properly converted in the crevices.

Finish with several coats of epoxy.

If you have a steel boat then this is a good bit of advice from Richard Phillips from the facebook site 'Live Aboard Steel Boats' for dealing with large areas of rust. I reprint this with his kind permission.

He says the 'best' treatment is grit blasting to SAE3 with two-part epoxy primer within an hour or so of blasting, then epoxy top coats (or even better, glass flake epoxy) with all paints sprayed.

That is however extremely messy and possibly expensive.
At the opposite end of the complexity scale and surprisingly long lived, I would consider something like this:
User wire brush on angle grinder to remove all flakes. Hoover up. Treat with vactan or fertan, (These both seem to be based on phosphoric acid, but check out their web-sites) allow to dry and lightly brush off dust. Then paint with a 50 /50 mix of Owatrol and linseed oil to soak into all the crannies. This will completely kill the rust and will last for years unless there is sitting salt water. After a while you could overpaint with an oil-based paint but there is no great rush.
Or instead of paint, smear with bilge grease as used by the Dutch - looks a bit like Vaseline, never sets and lasts for decades unless there is standing water.
If the areas are not huge, you can keep an eye on them I would go for the second approach as it is quick, cheap, easy to maintain and does not cause huge disruption. Keep a bottle of the owatrol / linseed mixture on the boat and you can always spot treat any bits that look a bit iffy before the rust takes hold.

All in all, if the rust you are seeing does not look too serious it should be quite easy to keep on top of.

HOLDING TANKS IN A STEEL BOAT

I own a steel boat. I like the added strength and security and the ease they can be repaired. Damage by hitting rocks is usually dents that can be beaten out and welded whereas this sort of impact could result in a write-off for a plastic boat.

However, there was one thing I definitely did not like the idea of – the holding tanks for grey and black water being part of the keel! Not a good design philosophy.

Particularly in a black tank the corrosion, unseen, can be severe because of the chemicals including uric acid (that comes from pee).
Honestly, how often do we lift the evil lid off our black tank and check for corrosion? Out of sight – out of mind – particularly with smelly poo tanks.
Sure, in a perfect world and a black credit card I would periodical take her to my favourite boat yard, have them open the tank, have them shot blast to remove the rust and calcium, have them re-epoxy and smile as they give me the invoice.

However, we are human and probably on a budget - besides life on deck with a G&T is so much nicer.

So instead I used to fret and worry.

Then a solution!

Why not construct, or have made, a plastic tank that fits within 20mm of the hull sides.

My initial thoughts were to fill the void with oil or grease as you can see in the sketch.

That worried me on environmental issues – so some thought. After a lot of testing and experimenting, I have chosen to use a cheap, basic, car antifreeze.

Environmentally friendly, and if there is ever a reason to work on this section of the keel then relatively clean.

<u>What concentration to use?</u>

I cut three test pieces of steel. On each one I left half with the original coating of red rust and then ground the other half to a shiny finish.

I the put each one in a glass jar with a mix of (a) pure undiluted antifreeze (b) 20% mix and (c) a 10% mix.

After two months I checked the results and was astonished.

All the steel samples looked as they had been ´pickled´ the rust had dropped away and the shiny area was dull grey with no sign of rust.

20%

30/3/20

The undiluted strip was the cleanest followed, as one would expect by the 20%, and then the 10%.

From these results I elected to use the 20% mix.

I then packed as much polystyrene sheet as I could in the gap to reduce the amount of liquid I would have to use.

Result, no more rust or worry or having to shot blast and epoxy every x number of years. The following illustration explains the basic idea.

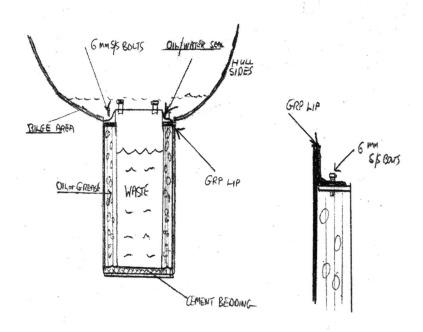

First task is to measure very carefully the size of the tank that will fit within the keel — also checking the width of the doors so you can get the finished tank into position when it is made.

My particular tank requirement was 90cm high x 50cm wide x 55cm. long

(The 50cm was the maximum width of the cabin door) this gave me a capacity of around 238 litres. Adequate but a lot less than the original tank. I did have the washing machine discharging into the tank to act as a 'flush' but have now added a diverter valve so I can choose, when conditions are correct, to pump directly overboard.

At this point you can choose between a custom manufactured plastic tank supplied by, for example www.tek-tank.com, they are based in England and are happy to quote for delivery worldwide. I have used this company before and they do make excellent products. Look at their website. The quote for this, with tax and carriage, was around €1,000. A super tank I am sure, replete with a five-year guarantee, but outside my budget.

As I already had a supply of glass mat and resin, I decided to make my own tank. It was quite a job, as with anything to do with boats it always takes longer and costs more than your first estimate - so be prepared.

I would guess that if I had to buy the glass and resin for a tank of this size it would cost in the region of €100, so quite a saving on a custom-built tank; albeit a lot of work

First construct a mold. To do this obtain relatively cheaply some laminated chip board and construct a box allowing for the thickness of the glass fibre, around 5/6 layers

Now some tips. It is best to make the box from smaller pieces of board joined on the inside with scrap pieces. The reason is that it is much easier to break out the mould bit by bit if in smaller pieces. And another idea that was blindingly simple; carefully cover the entire assembly in parcel tape. This proved to be a brilliant anti-stick surface when the time comes to remove the tank from the mold.

I also constructed the lid from a separate mold and glassed this into position.

The inspection hatch on my arrangement was 8mm Perspex left over from another project. Not particularly clever, true one can observe the level of the tank when clean, but I don't expect it to stay that way – no, the real reason was this was already in stock – it does look neat though.

Glass Fibre tank ready to fix.

To keep the base of the tank stable bed it in a sand/cement with added PVA adhesive - very cheap, waterproof and allows quite a lot of elasticity when fitting. Pour this into the keel just before fitting and with a 'squiggly' motion bed the tank firmly down.

Depending on your own setup work out a way to keep the tank secure from the top. On my installation I added a glass fibre lip that I bolted through using M6 stainless screws.

Now I can stop fretting about my keel dropping off and sit on deck with a G&T without guilt – another job done.

Cheers

The Dream

My yacht DriKe: a still September morning in the Mar
Menor, Spain

Thank you for reading this book.

I have enjoyed writing this and sharing some ideas.

Remember when we buy a boat, we are buying a dream. The reality can be somewhat different. But we still hold onto that dream. Some of these ideas will truly make your boat better and easier to live on.

I have already published a number of books on vastly different subjects. Please visit my website.

www.ChrisSouthwood.com/books

MY CONTACT DETAILS

If you have any questions, suggestions or critique please feel free to email me Mail@ChrisSouthwood.com
I promise to reply as soon as possible.

Now, dear reader, if you got this far, I assume you liked this book. As an independent publisher your feedback and star ratings are very important to us 'Indies' (Independent authors) and is much appreciated.

Just takes a couple of minutes on Amazon.

So happy boating, have a great time and buy loads of books.

Chris Southwood
Yacht DriKe
Almerimar
2020

Printed in Poland
by Amazon Fulfillment
Poland Sp. z o.o., Wrocław

64205038R00049